What is Creativity?

Originality, art & invention

John King

Light Press

*A catalogue record for this book is available
from the British Library*

ISBN: 978-1-907962-17-2

Published by Light Press

Reading, England

For Roxy

Contents

Preface

This book explores the concept of creativity. What is creativity? Is creativity something which solely exists in the human realm? Do non-human animals possess the attribute of creativity? Could the entire universe be pervaded with creativity?

I will be suggesting that the key to identifying instances of creativity is the identifying of instances of originality. I will then propose that works of art are not instances of originality but that human inventions are. Finally, I suggest that there are instances of originality in the non-human realm.

Introduction

What does it mean to talk of 'creativity'? Creativity is surely the ability to create – to bring forth things from the realm of inexistence into the realm of existence. The bringing forth of a thing is a spatio-temporal event which means that creativity occupies a spatio-temporal window. Furthermore, creativity surely entails originality; mere repetition of what already exists doesn't entail creativity. This means that creativity is the bringing forth of original things from the realm of inexistence into the realm of existence within a spatio-temporal window. This definition surely gets to the heart of the concept of creativity.

However, the delineation of which things are genuinely original when they enter the realm of existence is problematic; it is easy to consider a bringing forth to be an instance of originality when it is actually wholly devoid of originality. The classification of the bringing forth of things into instances of originality and instances lacking originality is the subject of this book.

In *Chapter One* I consider whether works of art are instances of originality and I conclude that they are not. In *Chapter Two* I consider whether inventions are instances of originality and I conclude that they are. In *Chapter Three* I reflect on whether there are inventions in the non-human realm and I conclude that such inventions exist. In *Chapter Four* I consider the possibility that the universe could be pervaded with instances of originality which exist in very wide spatio-temporal windows. Finally, in *Chapter Five* I draw some conclusions.

Chapter 1

Works of art

Let us first consider the poet. Imagine a person who writes a poem about a particular landscape. Most people would assert that this person is engaged in creativity; they are bringing forth an original work of art from the realm of inexistence. Whilst most people would also surely assert that it would not be true to say that the photocopying of this poem is an act of creativity. The act of photocopying is a bringing forth of things from the realm of inexistence into the realm of existence, but it is not an act of originality.

This position seems to have a certain intuitive appeal but is actually problematic. Let us consider a scenario in which the process of photocopying causes a mark to appear on one of the copies of the poem which the reader of the photocopy takes to be a comma. In this scenario we do not have a case of mere repetition but we have a new poem, an original work of art which due to the placement of the 'comma' may give rise to a profound new meaning to the poem. Should we consider this new poem to be the result of creativity? There is no doubt that this new poem is as much a bringing forth of an original work of art from the realm of inexistence to the realm of existence as the original. However, it would surely be an insult to the term to refer to this bringing forth as an act of creativity. If the bringing forth of the new poem is not an act of creativity, which it surely is not, then we have to ask what it is about the bringing forth of the original poem that endows this event with creativity. If we cannot find an acceptable answer then we might have to conclude that the bringing forth of the original poem itself is not a creative event.

Let us consider an alternative scenario in which the original poem is not brought forth from the realm of inexistence by a human. In this scenario the poem is brought forth when a box of lettered tiles

15

fall off a shelf due to the force of gravity and the letters fall onto the floor in a way that gives rise to the words and structure of the poem; for the sake of plausibility we can assume that it is a very short poem. Is this bringing forth an instance of creativity? As with our 'comma' scenario this event is surely a bringing forth of an original work of art from the realm of inexistence into the realm of existence. However, as with the 'comma' scenario, this too is surely not an instance of creativity.

One may want to resist the claim that the poem which results from lettered tiles falling to the ground in the manner described is the bringing forth of a work of art. Why would one want to do this? The 'falling tile' scenario entails the bringing forth of exactly the same original poem that we initially considered as being brought forth by the pen of the poet. If a person entered the room sometime after the tiles fell into place and observed the tiles they would assume that they are arranged that way as a result of a creative act. In other words, they would consider the letters to be a poem – a work of art. This raises the question of what a work of art is. Is a work of art something which is knowingly created to be a work of art? Or, is a work of art simply an arrangement of stuff which is ascribed to be a work of art by a person who perceives this arrangement?

If an arrangement of stuff only becomes a work of art if it is ascribed to be so by a perceiver – as occurs in the case of the observer in the 'falling tile' scenario – this means that the bringing forth of a poem, however it is brought forth, is not an instance of originality. In other words, there would be as much originality in the 'falling tile' scenario as in the 'poem brought forth by the poet' scenario, and there is no originality in the 'falling tile' scenario. So, the poet would not be engaged in originality when they bring forth an arrangement of letters and marks that simply contain the possibility of being interpreted as a poem. In this scenario there is no meaningful sense in which works of art can be said to be either instances of a bringing forth of creativity or to have a perception-independent existence. A work of art only exists if someone decides to call an arrangement of marks and letters, or an arrangement of stuff, a 'work of art'. This ascription is a very different thing from creativity, which is a bringing forth of originality within a spatio-temporal window.

One might want to resist the conclusion that the poet is not engaged in creativity. In order to do this one could claim that works of art are not things which are ascribed to be a work of art by a perceiver. Rather, one could claim that a work of art is something that is knowingly produced to be a work of art. However, this claim has bizarre consequences.

Let us consider the possibility that the poet is convinced that they are creating a work of art as they arrange the letters and marks in a particular pattern.

Does this conviction make the resulting arrangement of letters and marks a bringing forth of
originality? It surely does not. Consider an alternative scenario in which I am convinced that I am
bringing forth a work of art when I put a cup on a
table. I could position the cup very carefully to
enhance the overall visual impression of looking at
the 'cup and table'. This particular 'cup and table'
arrangement, as a work of art, would be a bringing
forth of an original thing from the realm of inexistence if this particular arrangement, including the
size and position of the cup, had not been brought
forth previously. However, this is surely not an act of
originality. If one accepted that it was then one
would also have to accept that any change that a

human makes to the universe, however small, could also be a work of art – a creative bringing forth of originality. It is surely the case that moving a cup a few millimetres across a table can never meaning-fully be described as an act of creativity.

So, if one claims that a work of art is something that is knowingly produced to be a work of art one ends up with this bizarre conclusion. Furthermore, there is another strong argument as to why this claim is wrong. The argument is simply that the claim demands too much because we can imagine a person being creative without them having the knowledge that they are being creative.

Let us accept the premise that the poet is engaged in creativity and imagine possible scenarios in which a poet is writing a poem but they have no knowledge that they are writing a poem. If any of these scenarios could pertain in reality then this means that creativity is possible without a 'knowledgeable creative process'. One obvious scenario in which a person can write a poem without knowledge of what they are writing is when the person is hypnotised. Another obvious scenario is when a person is at a level of drunkenness at which they have no knowledge of what they are doing but they are still able to write. Another obvious but more controversial scenario is the phenomenon of 'automatic writing' where people supposedly write without awareness of what they are writing.

In all of these scenarios works of art are brought forth from the realm of inexistence into the realm of existence by a human without that human having knowledge of what they have done. However, a poem written by a drunken or hypnotised person who is unaware of what they are doing is surely as much an act of creativity as an identical poem brought forth into existence by a person who is aware of what they are doing. This means that knowledge of whether a creative process is occurring is not of any relevance to whether a creative process is actually occurring. So, even if we were to accept that the poet is engaged in creativity, a 'knowledge-able creative process' cannot be used to delineate the creative from the non-creative.

Let us recap. It has been argued that the poet is not engaged in originality because works of art are things with a perception-dependent existence – any arrangement of letters and marks, or things, could be taken to be a work of art. And to call any minor change in an arrangement of letters or things an act of originality would be an abuse of the term. We have explored the argument that the poet could be said to be engaged in creativity because they are undergoing a 'knowledgeable creative process' – a process which is absent in the 'comma' and 'falling tile' scenarios. However, we have seen that this argument fails because creativity does not require such knowledge, whilst such knowledge can exist in the absence of creativity itself. Paradoxically, a person might think that they are being creative when they are not, whilst they can be creative without knowing it.

This means that we cannot make any sense of the view that a poet who is aware that they are writing a poem is an instance of creativity, whilst the poem that is created in the 'comma' scenario is not an instance of creativity. This is because creativity does not require knowledge of the creative process and both scenarios entail the bringing forth of 'original' poems from the realm of inexistence into the realm of existence. Whilst both poems are 'original' their bringing forth isn't necessarily an instance of originality. The 'comma' scenario doesn't entail originality, so the analogous nature of the cases means that the poet is also not engaged in originality. Everything that has been said of the poet also applies to all artists. So, our conclusion is that works of art have nothing to do with creativity. To find the realm of creativity we need to shift our focus.

Chapter 2

Inventions

It has been argued that creativity entails the bringing forth of original things from the realm of inexistence into the realm of existence. This means that delineating which bringing forths are creative bringing forths requires an accurate conception of 'originality'. It has been argued that the bringing forth of a work of art is not an instance of originality due to the perception-dependent nature of a work of art. It has also been argued that the claim that if one is knowingly being creative then one must necessarily be engaged in a creative bringing forth is fallacious. This leaves us with the question of which bringing forths entail originality. It is surely the case that human inventions entail originality. The aim of this section is to specify what exactly an invention is and what delineates the bringing forth of an invention from the bringing forth of a work of art.

An invention is simply an arrangement of stuff which fulfils a particular function when it brings forth novel interactions. In contrast, a work of art is simply an arrangement of stuff. An invention is therefore delineated from a work of art by its novel interactive functionality. An invention is only brought forth into existence when the arrangement of stuff that is the invention fulfils its function for the first time. In so functioning the invention is bringing forth types of interactions that have not existed before, and it is doing so within a spatio-temporal window. If the types of interactions that exist when a particular arrangement of stuff is brought forth merely replicate previously existing types of interactions then the particular arrange-ment is not an invention.

So, the bringing forth of the wheel was an in-vention – an act of originality. This particular arrangement of stuff – a circular frame revolving on an axle – performs the function of enabling things to be more easily moved between different locations when it interacts with the surface of the Earth. The interactions which were generated by the bringing forth of the first wheel were novel – they had never existed before. Before the invention of the wheel things were often moved by dragging them across the surface of the Earth. The set of interactions that exist when a wheel moves along the surface of the Earth are very different to those that exist when something is dragged across the surface of the Earth.

Acts of creativity in a particular spatio-temporal window often lead to a plethora of acts of creativity in subsequent spatio-temporal windows. The bringing forth of the wheel enabled the subsequent bringing forth of the horse-drawn carriage. When the horse-drawn carriage was brought forth from the realm of inexistence this was also an act of originality. This invention entailed a novel set of interactions between the carriage itself, the surface of the Earth, and one or more horses, with the function of moving people and goods over considerable distances.

Of course, there has been a multitude of other creative bringing forths entailing the wheel including the bicycle, the automobile, the wheelbarrow, the wheelchair, and the airplane. All of these things are arrangements of stuff whose initial operations were instances of originality when they were brought forth from the realm of inexistence. When these things were used for the function for which they were created they all gave rise to sets of interactions which didn't exist before they were invented.

The bringing forth of the first automobile was clearly an instance of creativity, but what about every automobile that has been brought forth since? The key to creativity is originality, and the key to originality is the particular set of interactions that exist when a thing is fulfilling its function. This means that an automobile with a different set of such interactions will be a bringing forth of creativity, whilst an automobile with the same set of interactions will not. So, if one were to simply paint an automobile a different colour this would not be a creative bringing forth. It is when one changes the interactions that exist through changing the mechanical operation of the automobile that a creative bringing forth occurs.

Chapter 3

The non-human realm

It has been argued that human inventions are bringing forths from the realm of inexistence that entail creativity. So far we have not considered whether creativity exists in the non-human realm. Why might one believe that creativity is a uniquely human capacity? The reason is presumably that one might believe that creativity requires freedom and that whilst humans have freedom the non-human realm doesn't. However, in reality creativity and freedom are unrelated, so even if humans were the unique possessors of freedom it wouldn't follow that creativity doesn't exist in the non-human realm. Let us briefly consider why this is so.

In reality it is impossible to know whether a human has the ability to think and act in any way differently from which they actually think and act. In other words, it is possible that every thought and action of a human is wholly determined by forces beyond their control. This possibility means that one could argue that the human species might not be engaged in creativity because creativity requires the freedom to think and act differently. However, this is obviously wrong. Even if the human inventor was wholly determined in their thought and action by forces beyond their control they would still be engaged in creativity. This means that creativity and the ability to act differently are not related. So if the non-human realm lacks freedom this doesn't mean that it lacks creativity.

It has been argued that human inventions are instances of creativity when they are brought forth into the realm of existence. Are there also non-human inventions? An invention has been defined as an arrangement of stuff which fulfils a particular function when it brings forth novel interactions. This means that the chimpanzee who first shaped a twig into a tool and then used it for the purpose of interacting with an anthill to remove ants is an inventor – an initiator of a bringing forth of originality within a spatio-temporal window. Similarly, the first bird that brought forth a nest for the purpose of interacting with its eggs is an inventor. The nest is brought forth as an invention when it has novel interactive functionality; this occurs when the nest interacts with an egg. These animals are inventors engaged in instances of creativity.

Let us now consider animals themselves. The body of an animal such as a chimpanzee is full of organs – arrangements of stuff which fulfil particular functions and entail particular sets of interactions. For instance, a heart is an arrangement of stuff which when it is functioning entails a particular set of interactions in order to fulfil its purpose of pumping oxygen-rich blood to every living cell in the body. This means that when the first heart was brought forth into the realm of existence its functioning would have entailed the bringing forth of novel interactions. In other words, the heart is an invention whose bringing forth was an instance of creativity. Of course, this also applies to other organs such as the first lungs, kidneys, eyes, and ears.

When we consider plants we surely have to conclude that the bringing forth of photosynthesis in chloroplasts was an invention. Photosynthesis involves an arrangement of stuff which entails interactions between sunlight, water and carbon dioxide that generate sugar and oxygen, the purpose of which is to produce chemical energy. When we move further back in time we also have to conclude that the bringing forth of the first eukaryotic cell was an invention, as was the first living cell itself. The bringing forth of the first living cell entailed a novel set of 'metabolising' interactions the purpose of which was energy production. The bringing forth of the eukaryotic cell entailed a novel set of interactions due to the much greater complexity of its metabolising interactions; the purpose of this cell was to increase the efficiency of energy production. Our conclusion has to be that the whole of the living realm has been brought forth through a plethora of instances of creativity in a sequence of spatio-temporal windows.

Chapter 4

The differing spatio-temporal windows of creativity

It has been argued that creativity is the bringing forth of an invention within a spatio-temporal window. Most of the bringing forths that we have considered occupy a very small spatio-temporal window. This means that it was possible for an individual human to observe the spatio-temporal window of creativity that was open when the bicycle, the automobile, and the wheelchair were brought forth into the realm of existence. The 'spatio-temporal window' is the area of space-time that was involved in the set of novel interactions that were pertaining when the invention was fulfilling its function for the first time.

When we consider the realm of the non-human we have to consider the possibility that some inventions entail a spatio-temporal window of creativity that far supersedes the life of an individual human. This means that a human could be observing an instance of creativity without realising because they only perceive a tiny segment of the window. It could be simply a factor of the nature of our perception of the world that many bringing forths occur far too slowly for us to be able to observe them and realise that an instance of creativity is occurring. The identifying of large spatio-temporal windows of creativity is obviously even more problematic when we consider bringing forths that occurred in the distant past.

Let us consider what we call 'laws of nature'. When we perceive the world around us things appear to us to interact in accordance with these laws. However, it has to be possible that this appearance exists because we are viewing the world from such a tiny spatio-temporal window. In other words, the universe could contain spatio-temporal windows of creativity which are open for millions of years. Within these windows parts of the universe gradu-

41

ally come to interact with other parts of the universe in a different way giving rise to types of interactions which never existed before. These changes would be instances of creativity – of invention – which entail novel sets of interactions which span millions of years when they are first brought forth. The function of these sets of interactions would be to generate the conditions that enable other novel sets of interactions to be brought forth. So, what appear to us to be non-creative interactions that are worthy of the label 'laws' could actually be part of very slow creative processes.

From this perspective we can ask the question: What is the universe? The answer will be: A vast array of differing and overlapping spatio-temporal windows of creativity.

Chapter 5

Conclusion

We started with the question: What does it mean to talk of 'creativity'? It has been argued that this question has a straightforward answer: *Creativity is the bringing forth of original things from the realm of inexistence into the realm of existence within a spatio-temporal window.* However, within this definition lies the problematic issue of classifying exactly which bringing forths entail originality.

It has been argued that works of art are not creative bringing forths and that the only bringing forths which entail originality are inventions. An invention is simply an arrangement of stuff which fulfils a particular function when it brings forth novel interactions. This means that creativity can be redefined: *Creativity is the bringing forth of inventions from the realm of inexistence into the realm of existence within a spatio-temporal window.*

In exploring the non-human realm it has been argued that non-human animals are inventors. It has also been argued that bodily organs, plants, and living cells are all arrangements of stuff that are inventions. Furthermore, it has been suggested that the universe itself can intelligibly be argued to be comprised of a succession of inventions that have produced what we call 'laws of nature'. In other words, the universe can intelligibly be described as a vast array of differing and overlapping spatio-temporal windows of creativity.